Contents

Our Fragile Planet

Since the beginning of time, natural disasters have rocked our planet and its **environment**. Yet the natural world has a way of restoring its balance even after what seem to be major catastrophes. Plants and animals once adapted to the harsh conditions of Earth's many **ice ages**; they spread again when the temperature rose and the glaciers receded. Grasses and shrubs soon re-establish themselves in areas that have been completely burned by fires or swamped by floods. Even events that seem devastating, such as volcanic eruptions, are often just temporary 'blips' in the natural cycle of the environment. Seeds soon thrive in the **nutrient**-rich lava on the slopes of volcanoes, and vegetation gradually takes over once again.

While these natural events change the face of Earth, the real damage – often irreversible – to the balance of the environment comes from human activity. Although humans have had an impact on the environment for thousands of years, it is only in the last century that the problem has become critical. With wide-scale development, industries that **pollute** the air and water, the widespread burning of **fossil fuels** in cars and power plants, and powerful weapons that could destroy nearly all life, human beings are the most dangerous threats to Earth's environment. Today, **conservation** is high on the

Safeguarding
the Environment

LEARNING
RESOURCES
CENTRE

Sean Connolly

FRANKLIN WATTS
LONDON•SYDNEY

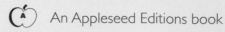 An Appleseed Editions book

First published in 2005 by Franklin Watts

Paperback edition 2007

Franklin Watts
338 Euston Road, London NW1 3BH

Franklin Watts Australia
Level 17/207 Kent Street, Sydney, NSW 2000

© 2005 Appleseed Editions

Appleseed Editions Ltd
Well House, Friars Hill, Guestling, East Sussex TN35 4ET

Designed by Helen James

ISBN 978 0 7496 7649 0

Dewey Classification: 333.72

A CIP catalogue for this book is available from the British Library

Photographs by The Barron Prize, Corbis (Alinari Archives, Theo Allofs, David Aubrey, David Ball, Bettmann, Alexander Burkatovski, Adrian Carroll; Eye Ubiquitous, INA FASSBENDER/Reuters, Darrell Gulin, Martin Harvey, George H. H. Huey, Hulton–Deutsch Collection, Charles Krebs, Lester Lefkowitz, Francis G. Mayer, David Muench, NASA/JPL/Handout/Reuters, Richard T. Nowitz, Stan Osolinski, Gabe Palmer, Reuters, Pete Saloutos, Paul A. Souders, TOUHIG SION/CORBIS SYGMA, Ron Watts), ESD, Getty Images (Walter Bibikow, EVARISTO SA/AFP)

Printed in China

Franklin Watts is a division of Hachette Children's Books

The spread of heavy industry has led to environmental threats affecting land, air, and water on Earth.

The Living Planet

Life exists on this planet because of a combination of factors that no other planet shares. Earth is the third planet from the sun. The inner two planets, Mercury and Venus, are far too hot to sustain life. The six planets beyond Earth are too cold. Even the nearest of these outer planets, Mars, has an average daytime temperature of -33°C or less. And because the Martian **atmosphere** is so thin, the night-time temperature can drop by more than 80°C.

Earth, by comparison, is protected by a thick atmosphere that contains the gases, such as oxygen and carbon dioxide, that animals and plants need to survive. The atmosphere also acts as a blanket, stopping warmth from escaping into space at night, and as a shield, causing most meteors to burn up. The '**ozone layer**' of the atmosphere protects Earth from harmful **radiation** from the sun but allows in the sunlight that is necessary for life. Water, the other essential ingredient for life, exists as a liquid only between 0°C and 100°C. Earth is the only planet on which the temperature is generally within this range.

list of international issues needing attention. Ignoring the problem is no longer an option because time is running out.

Facing Facts

Each year brings reports of new threats to the environment – global warming, the loss of the ozone layer, increased air and water pollution. Each of these is largely the result of human activity, and scientists predict serious dangers if such activity is not held in check or stopped altogether.

The campaign to safeguard the environment began about 200 years ago with a few lone voices identifying and predicting environmental destruction. It moved on to establish special areas to be protected from harmful human activity. But as new threats emerge – and existing ones continue to develop – the movement to protect the environment has tried to show how people's everyday lives and habits will need to change in order to prevent irreversible damage.

Number of Different Living Species by Type	
Type	Approximate Total
Bacteria	5,000
Algae and **Protozoa**	58,000
Fungi	47,000
Plants	248,000
Animals	1,033,000
TOTAL	1,391,000

Creating a Bad Atmosphere

The biggest man-made threats to the environment affect Earth's atmosphere and have far-reaching consequences. Global warming refers to the build-up of gases emitted when fossil fuels are burned. These fuels include the petrol used by vehicles as well as oil burned by industries. Carbon dioxide, methane and complex chemicals called CFCs (used in aerosol sprays and refrigerators) rise into the atmosphere and stop heat from escaping, causing a gradual rise in Earth's temperature. Even a small rise causes polar ice to melt, raising sea levels and threatening low-lying places around the world. Warmer temperatures might also lead to more dramatic storms as well as to permanent changes in climate and landscape. CFCs have also been blamed for damaging the ozone layer. Without this protective layer, people face a greater risk of developing skin cancer, and many important crops could be destroyed.

Rich Variety

Some parts of Earth are much richer in plant and animal life than others. The areas closest to the equator, especially the dense rainforests of South America, Africa and Asia, have the widest variety of life forms. Abundant rainfall and constant warm temperatures help thousands of species to thrive.

Statistics prove this clearly. For example, scientists counted more than 1,000 different species of trees growing in 2.5 square kilometres of rainforest on Borneo, an Asian island near the equator. By contrast, the entire land area of the United States and Canada – a region of about 19 million square kilometres – is home to only about 700 different species of trees.

Many animals, such as the lesser panda of the Himalayas, are native to only one part of the world. Major changes to its mountain habitat would threaten the panda population.

Unfortunately, the countries that have the most influence in world business and politics – especially the United States and western Europe – are located far from these rich ecosystems. Voters in these countries – who might demand conservation if the destruction was on their doorstep – often do not realize how many thousands of hectares of rainforests have been cleared to provide timber or to create grazing land for cattle destined to become fast-food hamburgers. Millions of trees have been lost and, with them, the ability to produce oxygen, which animals need for life, and to soak up carbon dioxide, which can cause many long-term environmental problems.

'The world has cancer, and that cancer is man.'

Merton Lambert, former spokesman for the Rockefeller Foundation.

The Damage Begins

From the earliest times, when human beings first discovered fire and developed tools, people have been changing the face of the planet permanently. Most of the earliest changes came about as people cleared trees from the land to create settlements and farms. Widespread clearances disrupted nature's way of locking good soil in place with the roots of trees.

Thousands of years ago, the low-lying plains of northern China and what is now Iraq were changed permanently after forests were cleared. Without trees and other vegetation to drink up the rain, water flowed downhill and flooded the plains. These man-made floods caused much of the best soil to be washed away, robbing farmland of nutrients and clogging rivers with **silt**. Uncontrolled grazing by livestock, coupled with the cutting down of trees and brush for firewood, resulted in the loss of valuable land in Africa and allowed the Sahara Desert to become huge.

Some landscapes have been marked by humans for many years. This Chinese farmer ploughs a rice field using methods that have not changed in centuries.

People's understanding of the planet and the effect they were having on it was limited throughout much of human history and prehistory. If farmland became poor because it had lost its nutrients, the earliest

agricultural settlements simply moved on to find new places to grow crops and raise livestock. Later, farmers found new ways to irrigate, or provide water for, dry lands and to drain marshes and other wetlands. They were unaware that, in doing so, they were destroying the natural **habitats** of many plants and animals.

Summer, by 16th-century Italian artist Francesco Bassano, shows humans thriving because of the natural riches surrounding them.

Wider Damage

Until the second half of the 18th century, the way of life for most people had remained largely unchanged for centuries. Most people lived in villages and conducted their lives within a small area. These rural labourers worked on small farms, which provided food for the villagers. Other things that people needed – such as tools, furniture and clothing – were handmade by villagers who worked in their own small houses or cottages.

The **Industrial Revolution**, which began in Great Britain in the late 18th century, changed this system dramatically. New manufacturing techniques made it possible to produce goods such as clothing and tools quickly and in large numbers. Factories sprang up as businesspeople saw the chance to increase profits dramatically. New agricultural machinery, such as mechanized planters and harvesters, meant that fewer workers were needed on farms. Labourers in Britain and other industrial countries moved from rural farms to cities and towns.

Workers remove the natural colour from large amounts of textiles in this 18th-century English bleaching mill, typical of the new type of factory spawned by the Industrial Revolution.

Salmon slump

Even in the early years of the Industrial Revolution, some observers began to make the connection between uncontrolled industry and damage to the environment. Scottish author John Naismith observed the changes in Hamilton Parish, near the growing industrial city of Glasgow, throughout the 1790s. He wrote about these changes in his book, *Thoughts on Various Subjects of Industry Pursued After in Scotland*. Naismith took a special interest in salmon, a fish long associated with Scottish rivers. He noted a sharp decline in their numbers, especially in the River Clyde, which flows through Glasgow. Part of the reason, he wrote, was simply that Glasgow's growing population included anglers who were catching more salmon. Looking more closely, though, he noticed that salmon **spawning grounds** were either altered or blocked completely by 'manufacturing machinery' along the river. With no place to breed, the salmon were dying out.

Johnny Appleseed

One of the most popular legends of the American frontier was based on a real person whose reputation helped build the belief that human beings should live alongside nature rather than try to tame it completely. John Chapman (1774–1845) was born in Massachusetts and by his early twenties had become devoted to two causes – the Western expansion of the United States and the spread of apple trees, which had been introduced to North America from Europe, to newly settled areas. Beginning in western Pennsylvania and Ohio, Chapman tried to predict which areas would be settled next; then he planted apple trees in clearings in these areas. By the time the settlers arrived several years later, he could sell them apples as well as seedlings to plant.

Helping to establish apple orchards – and gaining the nickname 'Johnny Appleseed' in the process – did not necessarily make Chapman an environmental hero. He did, however, strive to live in harmony with both the environment and the Native Americans who already lived there, following their example of living off the land without destroying it.

The changes brought about by the Industrial Revolution were not simply economic and social. The environment itself was changed on a wide scale. Rivers were re-routed to power new factories, which often polluted the water with their waste. Smoke from burning coal, which had replaced wood as the fuel for the new revolution, belched from smokestacks and chimneys, creating deadly smog in many cities. The landscape itself suffered as industrial waste was dumped freely in the countryside. Those countries that had followed Britain's industrial example prospered, leading many people to believe that manufacturing was the key to an ideal future. Few people were willing to disagree.

Voices of Warning

Although the early 19th century was a time of growing industry in many countries, it was also a time when some people began to take more interest in the natural world. This change of outlook was not limited to **naturalists** and other scientists. Even the world of art and literature reflected a renewed love of nature. Painters and writers in Europe and North America, inspired by the **Romantic Movement** in the arts, saw rural life as superior to society in cities. For them, the ideal was an untamed landscape,

Mountain Landscape by German artist Caspar David Friedrich was typical of Romantic art – the majestic natural scene is almost untouched by humans.

unaffected by what they saw as the ugly appearance of factories. English poet William Blake, in his poem *Milton*, wrote about the 'dark **Satanic** mills' that were ruining the countryside of his native land. William Wordsworth, another English poet, wrote of 'the close and overcrowded haunts/Of cities, where the human heart is sick' in his long poem *The Prelude*.

A Better Understanding

The 19th century was also a time of scientific advances, many of which contributed to ideas about the environment. Scientists were bringing together ideas about how the different elements of our planet – plants and animals, land, air and water – were linked. For example, English naturalist Charles Darwin published his famous work, *On the Origin of Species by Means of Natural Selection*, in 1859. In it, he wrote about his theory that plants and animals **evolve**, usually in response to their environment. He believed that species change to adapt to changes in their surroundings. One type of British moth, for example, had developed darker colouring to blend in with the soot-covered plants and buildings that resulted from Britain's growing number of factories.

Other scientists, such as Alexander von Humboldt, examined why certain types of plants thrive in some parts of the world but not in others. Again, it became clear that changes to the natural landscape – often the result of human interference – had a direct effect on plant and animal life in an area.

The work of English naturalist Charles Darwin, shown here in the 1850s, advanced the understanding of how plants and animals survive and develop in their native habitats.

In 1866, German biologist Ernst Heinrich Haeckel first used the word **ecology** to describe the relationship between plants and animals and their physical environment. This new branch of science was concerned with the widest issues of how the environment changes – either naturally or because of human interference.

Tying Things Together

American writers and scientists were also influenced by the renewed appreciation of nature. Unlike their European counterparts, whose views of nature were touched with longing because their own countries were already becoming overcrowded, Americans had a huge, untamed continent on their doorstep. They were less concerned with regretting what had happened overseas than with ensuring that the same mistakes would not be made in America.

Professor Ernst Haeckel poses during an expedition to the Asian island of Borneo in 1880. Such scientific trips enabled Haeckel to observe the delicate balance of nature.

The first Americans to examine the state of nature came from New England, one of the few parts of the United States to have factories in the early 19th century. A group of writers and thinkers formed the **Transcendentalist** Club in Boston in 1834. Among them were writer Ralph Waldo Emerson, social reformer Margaret Fuller, minister Theodore Parker, educator Bronson Alcott and author and naturalist Henry David Thoreau.

This group of thinkers discussed many ways to improve life in their own country and set an example for the rest of the world in the process. Like the Romantics, they believed that nature was precious. Emerson took a religious view, believing that nature was eternal and that human beings shared in its divine spirit. He also believed that nature would eventually recover from the wrongs that human beings had inflicted on it. Although Thoreau also treasured the natural world, he was less hopeful about its future. In 1845, Thoreau moved to a hut by Walden Pond in Massachusetts, where he lived for two years. During that time, he sought to show that people could live independently and in harmony with nature, without the need for unnecessary manufactured goods. His book about the experience, *Walden; or, Life in the Woods*, was published in 1854. It remains an inspiration for many people campaigning to safeguard the environment.

A portrait of Henry David Thoreau, seven years after his ground-breaking Walden *was published.*

'Thank God, men cannot yet fly and lay waste the sky as well as the earth.'

Henry David Thoreau.

Stating the Problem Clearly

While Emerson, Thoreau and other American thinkers were considering the spiritual and personal importance of nature, it took another New Englander to describe the specific threats to the environment – and what could be done about them. In 1847, George Perkins Marsh addressed the Agricultural Society of Rutland County, Vermont. He talked about the damage that human beings were causing to the land, especially through **deforestation**. Marsh argued that forests should be managed carefully, using basic principles of conservation.

His famous speech to the group was published in the same year and became the basis for his book, *Man and Nature; or, Physical Geography as Modified by Human Action*, published in 1864. This book was the first to reveal how human activity could cause irreversible damage to the environment. In particular, he attacked farming practices that led to the destruction of wetlands, deforestation and the **extinction** of plants and animals. Marsh even foresaw that unchecked human activity could affect weather patterns.

A Losing Battle?

The first people to sound the environmental alarm were 'voices in the wilderness' – literally. Only a few people understood that Earth was precious and delicate and not something to be **exploited** indefinitely. For many others, exploitation spelled progress and prosperity, offering a chance to clear new land and create new jobs. The new factories arising from the Industrial Revolution depended on an increasing supply of raw materials. The richest countries were growing wealthier through industry and the trade that came with it.

A New Way of Life

Newly invented machinery that used steam power meant that the earth could be dug up, trees could be felled and rivers could be re-routed in order to clear land or provide resources for industry. Dynamite, invented by Swedish chemist Alfred Nobel in 1867, dramatically increased the rate at which rugged landscapes could be 'tamed' to make roads, railways or mines.

The Suez Canal, built between 1859 and 1869, was one of the triumphs of 19th-century engineering.

All of these developments enabled engineers to bring about changes that could only have been dreamed about in previous centuries. The first Suez Canal, linking the Indian Ocean with the Mediterranean Sea, had been built in the 13th century BC by the ancient Egyptians. This narrow canal lasted until the eighth century AD. It was only in 1867, using steam-powered machines, that engineers were able to complete a canal wide enough to allow the passage of ocean-going ships. The first **transcontinental** railway completed in 1869, linked the eastern coast of the US with the Pacific Ocean. The public greeted these and other major engineering projects with enthusiasm.

Australia, which had only been settled by Europeans for a few decades, expanded rapidly throughout the 19th century. Its vast area and ample natural resources – including hardwood forests and extensive grazing land – fuelled this expansion. New railway lines pierced the interior of the country. Between 1875 and 1891, they increased nearly tenfold to more than 16,000 km. They also allowed goods and people more than 800 km into the interior, a region that had been scarcely seen by white people. Mineral exploration also played a part: the Mount Bischoff site (in Tasmania) was the world's largest known tin deposit when it was discovered in 1871.

A 'forest' of oil wells joins the landscape at Titusville, Pennsylvania, where the world's first commercial oil wells were drilled in 1859.

Gold in Australia

Gold was discovered in New South Wales, Australia, in 1851, leading to a 'gold rush' similar to the one that had occurred in California only two years earlier. The young country saw a flood of hopeful immigrants rushing in, seeking to make their fortunes from gold. In the next decade, Australia's population tripled in size, owing in large part to the influx of gold-seeking immigrants.

What the gold hunters did not know – or simply ignored – was that the Australian environment was very delicate. Widespread mining involved clearing away brush and vegetation that held nutrients in the soil and provided food for grazing animals such as wallabies and

RIVER-BED CLAIM ON THE TURON.
to re-make the discovery,

kangaroos. Some observers, such as explorer William Howitt, noticed the environmental damage that the gold rush was causing. But their voices, like those of environmentalists in other parts of the world, were ignored by the people responsible for the damage.

'We had quietness and greenness, and the most deliciously cool water, sweet and clear. But this quietness and greenness cannot last. Prospectors will quickly follow us. . . . The hop-scrubs will be burned, the bushes in and on the creek cleared away, the trees on the slope felled, and the ground torn up for miles around. The **crystalline** water will be made thick and foul with gold-washing; and the whole will be converted into a scene of desolation and discomfort.'

Explorer and naturalist William Howitt, writing about Australia in the 1850s.

A Changing Continent

The development of railways in North America in the 19th century opened up much of the continent for new settlements. America's western expansion was one of the most significant reasons for the growth of the United States. Dense forests and open plains, once inhabited only by scattered tribes of Native Americans, were turned over to cultivation (raising crops). As a result, about 98 per cent of North America's native tall-grass prairies were eventually destroyed, along with half of its wetland areas and 98 per cent of its old-growth forests.

Slaughter for Fun

The widespread destruction of the environment in the 19th century went hand in hand with some equally extensive slaughter of wildlife. Much of this was because of what conservationists call 'habitat destruction'. Millions of native Australian animals died when scrub landscape and woodlands in the Outback were converted for cattle grazing.

The development of new technology – especially high-powered and accurate rifles – increased the effect. Bison, sometimes called buffaloes, were almost driven to extinction during this period in North America. Scientists estimate that as many as 60 million bison grazed on the Great Plains at the start of the 19th century. After just a few decades of 'sport' hunting, fewer than 1,000 bison roamed the plains by 1889. But they were saved from extinction and today about 30,000 bison live on protected areas in the West.

Mass hunting was not confined to North America. Hunters in Africa, armed with powerful rifles, and employing local people as servants, killed countless elephants, antelopes and other species. In Asia, tigers began to come under threat. In 1911, King George V took part in a hunt that killed 39 tigers in just 11 days.

Mounted 19th-century riflemen could pick and choose their 'trophy' bison from herds that numbered in the thousands.

The Birth of Conservation

The second half of the 19th century, a time often called the Victorian Era after the British queen reigning at the time, was a period of great advancement. New developments in electricity, transportation and communications boosted industrial development. Factories could produce even more goods than before, and factory owners knew that their products would find markets around the world. Natural resources such as timber, coal, gas and even water were often considered merely the necessary 'basic ingredients' of industrial progress.

An Age of Exploration

At the same time, a number of men ventured from their own countries in search of unexplored lands. Explorers crossed the deserts of Australia, the harsh mountains of Afghanistan and India, the frozen **tundra** of northern Canada and Siberia and the dense tropical forests of South America and Africa.

This early photograph shows a group of mountaineers crossing an Alpine crevasse in 1866, a time when expeditions and exploration captured world imagination.

By the beginning of the 20th century, expeditions were even making their way to the North and South Poles. Fewer and fewer places remained to be explored.

All of this exploration had profound side effects. One was the feeling that the world was losing some of its mystery. At the same time, people were becoming more aware of the dwindling natural environments around them. With trains and telegraph lines crossing once-impassable deserts and plains, and with forests being cleared at a dramatic rate, there was real cause for alarm. Worst of all, governments seemed to be approving and even encouraging these changes.

The Lower Falls make up just part of the natural marvels of Yellowstone National Park, created in 1872.

National Efforts

Setting themselves against these seemingly unstoppable trends, a number of individuals began working to conserve the environment. Conservationists tried to get local and national governments to protect special wilderness areas. The big breakthrough came in 1872, when the US Congress passed legislation making Yellowstone the first official national park in the world. This move was a landmark in conservation since it was the first example of environmental lawmaking on a national level. A **precedent** had been set, one that would serve as an example for conservationists not only in the US but also in other countries. But the establishment of America's first national park – and with it the promise of others – did not reverse the environmental trend. The same session of Congress passed the infamous Mining Law, which threatened large tracts of public land with wide-scale development.

'Unless means are taken by government to withhold them from
the grasp of individuals, all places favourable in scenery to recreation
of the mind and body will be closed against the great body of the
people . . . to simply preserve them as monopoly by individuals.'

Frederick Law Olmsted, American landscape gardener and naturalist who campaigned
for the establishment of Yellowstone and other national parks.

*New Zealand's Waipoua
Kauri Forest Reserve,
established in 1952,
protects the last traces
of what were once
extensive forests of kauri,
a type of pine.*

Building on Success

Conservationists used the publicity surrounding Yellowstone National Park to
make their views more widely known. In 1873, the American Association for the
Advancement of Science presented Congress with a **petition** calling for a ban
on the wasteful use of natural resources. This scientific interest helped establish
the **federal** forest reserves (later called national forests) in 1891 and the US Soil
Survey in 1899. In 1916, Congress established the National Park Service to take
care of the growing number of parks and protected areas.

Other countries followed this example. Canada established Banff National Park in
the Rockies in 1885. South Africa set aside land for the Kruger Game Reserve in
1898. Bunya Mountains became Australia's first national park in 1908.

John Muir

One of America's greatest crusaders for national parks, John Muir (1838–1914), was actually born in Scotland. Muir was still young when his family moved to the United States. He was fascinated by his new home and studied its geography and wildlife extensively, especially in the wilderness areas of the West. In 1868, he moved to the magnificent Yosemite Valley in California. Four years earlier, Congress had granted ownership of the valley to the state of California, provided that it was preserved as a park. Muir felt very protective about this unspoiled natural gem, and he began to campaign to safeguard it – and other wilderness areas like it – against further development. Together with Ansel Adams and other conservationists, he urged Congress to form a series of national parks that would be protected and maintained with government money. Their efforts eventually succeeded and, in 1890, Yosemite became one of three new national parks to be established in the US.

Britain's first national park was established nearly six decades later, in 1949

The John Muir National Historic Site in Martinez, California, preserves the works of one of the world's great environmentalist heroes.

Wake-up Calls

By the early 20th century, many people had accepted the need to protect unspoiled natural areas. Zoos and captive breeding programmes acted to save **endangered** animal species from extinction. Many countries set aside land in the form of national parks, forests and coastlines. Naturalists and other scientists explored wilderness areas, recording new species of plants and animals and studying how habitats operated. Although these actions – and the attitudes that drove them – helped preserve 'special' plants, animals and landscapes, they put less emphasis on the 'ordinary' places where people lived and worked.

Closer to Home

By the middle of the century, though, it was apparent that many towns and cities – away from popular national parks – were unhealthy and often polluted. Sometimes the difference between these two types of landscapes was stark and dramatic.

An oil-covered seabird is one of the many victims of the Torrey Canyon *wreck in 1967, when a stretch of the southern English coast was damaged by an extensive oil spill.*

Tugboats, barges and heavy industry had changed the look of the River Thames in London by the 20th century, bringing pollution as well as wealth to the British capital.

For example, Great Britain established its first ten national parks in the 1950s. These parks offered British people the chance to hike, camp and fish in a range of natural surroundings. But at the same time, British towns and cities were suffering from dangerous air pollution. Severe pollution in London claimed between 3,500 and 4,000 lives in 1952 and another 700 lives in 1962.

It was not surprising that Great Britain, a small island with a long industrial history, should suffer from some form of pollution. But these same decades saw pollution affecting other countries, including the United States. America's vastness, with its rolling prairies and open plains, was powerless to halt the spread of pollution. On Thanksgiving weekend in 1966, weather conditions around New York City trapped polluted air in the atmosphere, leading to 168 deaths.

But it was not just air pollution that grabbed headlines. In 1967, the oil tanker *Torrey Canyon* ran aground and broke up on the southern coast of England. About 106,000 tonnes of oil spilled out and devastated a wide stretch of shoreline. On January 31, 1969, an oil spill off the coast of Santa Barbara, California, closed beaches and caused enormous damage to marine wildlife. Just five months later, another dramatic pollution news story horrified the public. The Cuyahoga River in Cleveland, Ohio, had caught fire because so many chemicals had been dumped into it.

Anger and Energy

These dramatic events all took place at a time when many people – especially young people – were calling for social changes. People campaigned for peace,

Silent Spring

Every so often, a single book can sum up the goals of a wide-ranging campaign and help motivate people to take action. One such book was *Silent Spring* (1962), written by American **marine biologist** Rachel Carson. Using clear and persuasive language, Carson warned of the serious dangers posed by DDT and other chemical pesticides. She argued that such pesticides kill not only the insects they target, but also other forms of wildlife. Carson believed that birds that ate contaminated insects would no longer be able to reproduce successfully, and the title of her book referred to the absence of birdsong once bird populations had been destroyed by the chemicals.

Rachel Carson's ominous warnings were strengthened by her awareness of the 'food chain' that links poisoned insects to birds and other animals.

The book was published at a time when many people were questioning the actions of governments and businesses. By pointing out the delicate balance of nature and suggesting risks that humans could also face from dangerous chemicals, Carson captured the public's attention. Within a decade, DDT was banned in the US, the UK and many other countries. More importantly, other people were inspired to follow Carson's example in investigating the effects of human activities on the environment.

Saving the Grand Canyon

The Sierra Club was founded as a charity in 1892. American charities do not pay taxes on their income as long as they are not involved in politics. But by the 1960s, with the environment coming under repeated threats, the Sierra Club found it impossible to stay out of the political arena. In June 1966, it published full-page newspaper advertisements in *The New York Times* and *Washington Post*. The advertisements opposed plans to build a dam that would flood the Grand Canyon, one of the most recognizable natural wonders in the world. The advertisement said simply, 'This time it's the Grand Canyon they want to flood. The Grand Canyon.' The next day, the Sierra Club received news that it had lost its no-tax position but, at the same time, membership requests came flooding in. Ultimately, the campaign was successful. In 1968, the Grand Canyon dam plan was abandoned.

for ethnic and gender equality and for fairer treatment of poor countries. Protesters now began to demand that their governments take action to protect the environment. They took their cue not only from the news stories they saw on television, but also from scientific studies outlining the scope of the problem worldwide. With this extra publicity and support, longstanding conservation groups, such as the Royal Society for the Protection of Birds (RSPB), mounted campaigns focused on specific environmental targets.

Environmental scientists found that their reports, once read mainly by fellow scientists, were now being taken seriously by governments and voters. Seeing the problem globally, rather than as confined to one nation or region, they helped mobilize international support. One of the first results was the United Nations **Biosphere** Conference, held in Paris, France, in 1968. For the first time, scientists and lawmakers from around the world began working together and coordinating ideas on issues such as pollution, habitat destruction and conservation.

Active campaigns in the 1960s, led by America's Sierra Club, helped to preserve the fragile landscape of the Grand Canyon.

The Message Gets Through

The widespread social protests of the 1960s and 1970s taught environmental activists many lessons. One of the most important centred on the best way to press for lasting change. The advances in areas such as racial and gender equality – marked by permanent changes in countries' laws to preserve progress – showed that protests needed to become political. Only by persuading elected representatives to vote for conservation could the environmental movement gain ground. Moreover, laws could give real 'bite' to the gains. Individuals and companies could be fined for breaking environmental laws, just as employers could be punished for refusing to hire women or minorities.

Actions and Results

A number of environmental organizations were formed in the late 1960s and early 1970s. These included international groups like Friends of the Earth (1968)

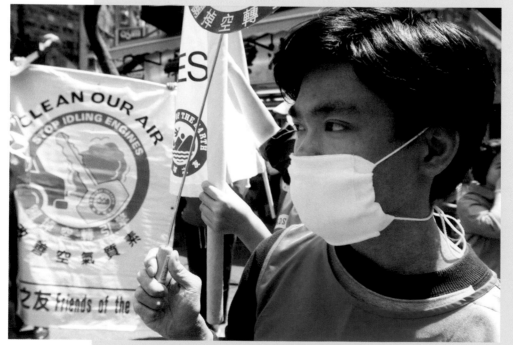

Many of the environmental action groups of the late 1960s have carried the message into the new century. Friends of the Earth protesters lead an anti-pollution demonstration in 2000 aimed at cutting car exhaust in Hong Kong.

and Greenpeace (1970), as well as national organizations such as America's Environmental Defense Fund (1967), and the National Resources Defense Council (1970). Other conservation groups, which had been in existence for decades, took on a more active role to reflect the charged political atmosphere.

British conservation groups, which had joined in the efforts to found the first UK national parks, continued to work to promote environmental causes. Groups such as the Youth Hostels Association, the Ramblers' Association, the Council for the Preservation of Rural England (CPRE) and the Council for the Preservation of Rural Wales (CPRW) continued to lobby the government for measures to protect – and allow access to – the countryside for the benefit of everyone. These causes proved popular, and politicians found it hard to ignore them for two important reasons. First, voters did not like the idea of landscapes being ruined and species facing extinction. Second, the issue of pollution (which was central to the whole environmental debate) threatened the health and even the lives of voters themselves.

'I wanted a demonstration by so many people that politicians would say, 'Holy cow, people care about this.' That's just what Earth Day did.'

Gaylord Anton Nelson, the 'Father of Earth Day'.

All of this grassroots activism began to show some results across the world. Many countries passed laws setting limits on industrial pollution and protecting endangered species. New government organizations, such as the

US Environmental Protection Agency (established in 1970), acted as public watchdogs. New political parties, devoted to the environmental cause, also sprang up. The United Tasmania Group was formed at a public meeting in Hobart, Tasmania (Australia's Island state) in March 1972. New Zealand's Values Party, dating from May 1972, became the world's first national party with environmental aims. Similar groups in other countries would eventually be called 'green parties', echoing the term that German environmentalists used in their first national-level election in 1980.

Progress also blossomed on the international level. The United Nations Environmental Program (UNEP) was formed at a UN-organized environmental conference in Stockholm, Sweden, in 1972. UNEP has since been seen as the 'environmental conscience of the United Nations' bridging the gap between the industrialized nations and **developing countries**.

The spread of farming has reduced the hunting range of the protected Ethiopian wolf. No more than a few dozen of these once widespread animals remain in the wild.

Official Protection

Environmentalists have long been concerned about the threats to endangered species of plants and animals. Rare flowers and trees are uprooted and used for furniture, timber, perfume and even food. Animals are shipped far from their native habitats to be eaten or kept as pets. The Convention (agreement) on International Trade in Endangered Species of Wild Fauna and Flora (CITES) was adopted in 1973. Since that time, it has restricted world trade in about 5,000 animal species and 25,000 plant species threatened with extinction.

The Father of Earth Day

The first Earth Day, on April 22, 1970, saw more than 20 million Americans protest about environmental destruction. Since then, Earth Day has become an international event, observed each year by millions of people around the world.

The idea for Earth Day can be credited to one man, Gaylord Anton Nelson. Nelson, born in 1916, grew up fishing and hiking among the woods and lakes of his native Wisconsin. In 1958, he became governor of Wisconsin. As governor, he recalled the 'rich land, clean air and safe water' of his childhood. In 1961, Nelson began a 10-year, $50 million programme to buy private lands and preserve them as wildlife and recreation areas. He funded this scheme through a penny-a-pack tax on cigarettes.

Nelson continued to promote environmental issues as governor and, from 1962, as a US senator. Unfortunately, other senators and representatives at the time had little interest in passing wide-scale laws to limit industrial output. Then, in late 1969, Nelson observed young people organizing informal lectures, called 'teach-ins', to build opposition to the war in Vietnam. He thought he could use a similar approach to educate people about the environment. The day set aside for these teach-ins would be called 'Earth Day'. According to Nelson, once the idea was born, the first Earth Day organized itself by word of mouth. It soon became the largest demonstration in history.

Australia's Coastal Gem

The Great Barrier Reef, one of the most outstanding natural wonders in the world, extends about 2,000 kilometres along the northeast coast of Australia. This coral habitat is formed from the skeletons of countless animals called polyps. More than 2,000 species of fish live on the reef. Noticing that the reef and its inhabitants were being threatened by wide-scale development, the Australian government established the Great Barrier Reef Marine Park in 1975. The park remains an example of how to balance tourism and other industries with the conservation of delicate marine habitats.

The Fish that Broke the Dam

Activists were quick to find ways to use new environmental protection laws to promote real change. One of the most influential examples came in the mid-1970s, and it centred on a small fish called the snail darter. In 1976, zoologist David Etnier, law professor Zygmunt Plater and student Hiram Hill filed a lawsuit to stop work on the Tellico Dam in Tennessee. A year earlier, Plater and Hill had used the terms of the new Endangered Species Act to get the US Department of the Interior to list the snail darter, which lives in the Little Tennessee River below the site of the proposed dam, as an endangered species.

On May 25, 1976, a judge ruled that it was too late to stop the project, which was nearly complete and had already cost the government $80 million. The case was taken to the US Supreme Court for a final ruling. On June 15, 1977, the Supreme Court ruled to suspend construction, with Chief Justice Warren Burger explaining, 'It is clear that Congress intended to halt and reverse the trend toward species extinction whatever the cost'.

Emergency Action

The oil tanker *Arrow* ran aground in Chedabucto, Nova Scotia, in 1970, spilling its cargo along a stretch of beautiful coastline. Canadians were shocked by the environmental damage and the delayed response in dealing with it. Many people demanded an environmental emergency system that could be put into action as soon as a crisis developed.

Three years later, Environment Canada, a branch of the Canadian government, formed just such a system when it set up national and regional committees known as Regional Environment Emergency Teams (REETs). Each

REET has members drawn from the government's environmental departments and from private industry. The REETs have two main responsibilities: to plan effective responses to a wide range of emergencies and to put these plans into action when there is a crisis. In times of emergency, the REET acts as a team of experts, offering constructive advice to the On Scene Commander (OSC) in charge of the response.

Quickly mobilized and having a real stake in the environment, REETs have helped Canada deal with oil spills, chemical fires, oil rig explosions and other environmental crises.

A volunteer helps in the clean-up operation after the break up of the oil tanker The Prestige *along the northwest coast of Spain in early 2003. The Spanish government estimated that the oil spill caused damage valued at more than $1 billion.*

New Tactics and Old Ideas

Some activists believe that attention-grabbing actions are the only way to attract and hold the public's interest in the environmental cause. They are prepared to take their protests as far as the law allows – and sometimes even further – in order to gain wider attention. Others look to the traditional beliefs of people such as Native Americans and Australian **Aboriginals** as examples of how humans should coexist with the environment.

Mixed Results

Well-publicized campaigns to save specific wetlands, desert landscapes, mountains or even individual plant and animal species certainly help to promote the environmental movement. A single event, watched by millions on television, can lead to donations of time and money for environmental organizations. It can also become an issue in local and national elections.

Protesters concerned with a wide range of environmental and other issues demonstrate outside the G8 meeting of powerful world leaders in Evian, France, in June 2003.

Nuclear Power

For decades, many scientists recommended nuclear power as an alternative to fossil fuels to meet the world's energy needs. They argued that nuclear power plants did not pollute the atmosphere or use up supplies of coal and oil. But nuclear energy has its own risks and can become very dangerous in the event of an accident. Two major nuclear accidents within seven years of each other turned many people against this form of energy production.

The first occurred at the Three Mile Island nuclear reactor in Pennsylvania in 1979. A combination of breakdowns led to damage amounting to $1 billion, although the public was not directly endangered. But in 1986, an accident at a nuclear power plant in Chernobyl, Ukraine, released dangerous radiation into the atmosphere. More than 30 people were reported killed at the time, and radiation sickness has been blamed for a number of deaths since then.

Widespread publicity does not always help a cause, however. Heartfelt protests and demonstrations can sometimes turn into riots. People watching such images on television are often disgusted by the violent behaviour, and the point of the protest is lost. The anti-**globalization** protest at the 2003 international economic **summit** in Seattle, Washington, was a good example of this. Protesters set out to demonstrate against **multinational** businesses such as

The Three Mile Island nuclear reactor, photographed on March 28, 1979, the day of its nuclear accident.

Champions of Direct Action

Greenpeace was founded in 1971 in Vancouver, Canada, by activists who opposed US military tests of nuclear weapons in Alaska. Since then, it has gained attention and followers because of its daring protests. Greenpeace activists have disrupted whaling expeditions and baby seal culls (organized killings), often standing between animals and hunters with harpoons or guns. They have also climbed the outside of city skyscrapers to hang prominent protest banners.

Perhaps the most dramatic – and tragic – action involving Greenpeace came in 1985. The Greenpeace ship *Rainbow Warrior* was on its way to stage protests about French nuclear weapons testing in the Pacific Ocean. While in port in New Zealand, the *Rainbow Warrior* sank mysteriously, and its photographer, Fernando Pereira, drowned. It was later proved that the ship had been deliberately sunk by French military agents using explosives. The tragedy gained many supporters for Greenpeace, and the scandal led to the resignations of French Defence Minister Charles Hernu and Admiral Pierre Lacoste, director of the French Secret Service.

The Greenpeace ship Rainbow Warrior *docked at Sydney, Australia, before the mysterious attack in 1985.*

fast-food chains and agricultural companies, which they believe exploit countries and their environments. Although some observers might have been won over to this view, for many people the lasting image from Seattle is not the anti-globalization message, but rather the ugly clashes between protesters and the police.

Victory for Older Traditions

Environmentalists have looked at the beliefs of several **pre-industrial** cultures for inspiration in balancing development and conservation. People such as Native Americans, Canada's **First Peoples**, and Australian Aboriginals maintain strong traditions of preserving their natural surroundings, which they consider sacred. Environmentalists have supported the efforts of these people to gain more of a say in how their land is treated.

In 1985, the Aboriginal people of Australia's Northern Territory regained ownership of Uluru (formerly known as Ayers Rock), Australia's most recognizable natural feature, from the federal government. The Aboriginals then leased it back to the Australian National Parks and Wildlife Service. Under the new arrangement, however, park officials and visitors have to comply with regulations honouring the site's sacred status in Aboriginal culture.

In May 1992, following a land-claim victory by the Inuit people (the first inhabitants of Northern Canada), the Canadian government agreed to a plan to carve 2 million square kilometres from the Northwest Territories. After seven years of political planning, this land became a new Canadian territory, known as Nunavut (Inuktikut for 'our land').

A young Australian Aboriginal boy watches as his father carves a boomerang.

Go Climb a Tree

On December 10, 1997, a 23-year-old Californian woman named Julia Butterfly Hill climbed a 55-metre redwood tree known as Luna. The Pacific Lumber/Maxxam Corporation had planned to fell the 1,000-year-old tree and the surrounding forest. Risking death, Hill vowed to stay in the tree until the company guaranteed to save it. Surviving in a makeshift shelter among the branches and relying on food hoisted to her by supporters, she forced a standoff that lasted more than two years. Eventually, the company agreed to save the tree and a 2.2 hectare area surrounding it. On December 18, 1999, Hill finally climbed down from Luna and was hailed as an environmental heroine.

The Local Level

Like many old sayings, the phrases 'charity begins at home' and 'all politics is local' still mean something in the modern world. They express the view that social and political change on a national or international level can often be traced to actions and opinions in small communities or even within a household. This principle can certainly be applied to the ongoing effort to safeguard the environment.

Raising Awareness

The first step in bringing about lasting change on a wider scale is to raise awareness, convincing individuals of the importance of the issue. For example, many of the important changes in the modern world – gender and racial equality, health warnings about smoking or rights for the handicapped – have been achieved because activists worked to raise people's awareness about the issues. Environmental activists have been working to raise awareness for more than four decades, and people can now see many of the results.

Greenpeace organized the free distribution of special, cleaner diesel during a well-publicized fuel shortage in Great Britain in 2000.

Children today learn safe practices in wooded areas to prevent devastating forest fires. Campaigns and even laws (with associated fines) have led to a decline in the number of people who litter. **Recycling** programmes – concentrating on glass, paper, aluminium, and other materials – have helped to curb the rapid increase of waste material in the world.

Some of the most important campaigns have been aimed at children. Young people can easily understand the environmental message and can help bring about change. Local branches of environmental organizations often send representatives to schools to spread the word about conservation. Special projects and contests, organized locally or nationally, also promote a sense of awareness among young people. These programmes pass on detailed information

Mountains of paper that would otherwise have be buried or burned await pulping, the first stage of recycling paper for future use.

about environmental concerns and how individuals can help to deal with them. Local award winners, whose achievements are publicized in the newspapers and on the Internet, become ideal role models for others who are interested in playing a part in the environmental campaign.

Parents can play an important role by teaching young children about recycling and other home-based environmental efforts.

The message hits home

One of the best ways to build awareness of environmental issues is to target those people who will be in charge of the Earth in the future – children. What children learn today can affect not only their own families and communities, but also how these same communities (and countries) will take major decisions in the future.

A new school-based scheme in Australia gives children the chance to learn about all sorts of environmental issues. The Gould League, one of the country's leading conservation groups, has introduced the Professor WasteWise programme to take the environmental message to schools. Middle schools across Australia can be visited by experts who introduce children to the whole subject of waste management. These programmes, which feature lively in-school presentations, can be tied in with existing schemes in schools and communities. Children come out with a greater knowledge of the problems – and a real enthusiasm for finding new solutions for the future.

Environmental awards

Each year Australian schoolchildren have the chance to win money and prizes for their schools by competing for the Hands on for Habitat Awards. The awards competition takes place in the run-up to Australia's annual Threatened Species Day (7 September). Children can use their curiosity and skills to complete detailed entries in the competiton. Along the way, they learn about – and help – Australia's threatened plant and animal species. They find out about the threats to these species – including habitat destruction, hunting, intensive farming and even competition from non-native species such as cats, dogs and rats.

The Hands on for Habitat Awards supply schools and teachers with resource kits and guidelines about how best to complete entries. At the same time, they themselves might be learning for the first time about the threats facing the natural world around them.

Children have the chance to see artworks of their winning entries used in posters and other promotional materials for the national campaign.

Similar contests and awards have raised the profile of the environmental cause elsewhere in the world. Eighteen-year-old Whitney Boulton was one of five 2003 winners of the annual Gloria Barron Prize for Young Heroes, which recognizes exceptional young Americans who have made a significant positive difference to people and the planet. Whitney achieved dramatic results in her home town in New York State. Passing a stagnant stream that her father remembered as once being full of life, she decided to clean it up. She organized a 'stream team' to help with the job. Equipped with gloves, boots and rubbish bags, more than 50 young volunteers cleaned a 5-kilometre stretch of stream. They removed car tyres, shopping trolleys, bicycles and even an old refrigerator.

Looking Ahead

Some people despair when they think of what is in store for the environment in the future. It can sometimes seem as if there is no end to the crises that loom on the horizon: global warming, loss of the ozone layer and over-population.

But most of these problems can still be addressed and controlled – if not reversed. What the world needs is a new way of thinking that will draw countries together to solve shared problems. The Kyoto **Protocol**, established in 1997, is a plan to reduce the output of **greenhouse gases** in several countries. However, the protocol will become a binding treaty only when countries producing 55 per cent of these gases – mainly Russia and the US – sign it. Bowing to international pressure, Russia signed the protocol in September 2004. The United States, however, continues to refuse to sign it. President George W. Bush has stated repeatedly that the United States would lose thousands of jobs if US industries were forced to reduce their greenhouse gas output.

German Chancellor (Prime Minister) Gerhard Schroeder addresses 'Renewables 2004' an international conference for renewable energies held in Bonn, Germany, in June 2004.

A robot vehicle, the Sojourner Mars Rover, uses scientific equipment to test Martian rock as part of the Pathfinder mission in 1997.

Countries can also work together by sharing information about new energy production methods that are less harmful to the environment. Burning oil and other fossil fuels became the most common method of producing energy at a time when these fuels were plentiful and inexpensive. As supplies have decreased – and as political uncertainty has clouded many oil-producing nations such as Iraq – the cost of oil has increased. The threat of future low supplies and high costs has prompted scientists to explore alternative sources of energy. Some of these sources, such as solar power, wind generation and tidal power, are limitless in supply and do not pollute the environment. For years, they were considered too expensive compared with oil. Perhaps they will become more attractive as fossil fuels become scarcer and more costly.

Opposite Approaches

The nations of the world can choose a number of different paths to address the increasing threats to the environment. Two approaches sum up the range of possibilities. The most dramatic is to look to other planets to settle and develop. Scientists are considering how to make another planet – the usual choice is Mars, since its conditions are most like those of Earth – habitable for plants

and animals. Before that could happen, scientists would have to trigger many changes in the Martian atmosphere to make it thick enough to hold air and liquid water. This process, which would be time-consuming and expensive, is called terraforming.

The other extreme is based on the fact that, for the foreseeable future, the world population will continue to increase and poorer countries will continue to build new industries. This environmental approach accepts these facts but tries to balance development with **sustainability**. It tries to provide light, heat and power to cities and factories without using up fossil fuels, emitting carbon and other material into the atmosphere or polluting the water and landscape.

Whatever the approach, finding solutions to the environmental problems facing our planet needs to be the goal for world leaders in the 21st century. Only by working together can the world community face the challenge of safeguarding the environment – before it is too late.

Huge panels point upwards to receive maximum sunlight before turning it into electricity at a solar energy plant.

Sustainable Development

Many activists blame businesses for all of the world's environmental troubles. Some businesses, however, are committed to changing the environment for the better. One such company is Energy for Sustainable Development (ESD), which advises other companies, cities, towns and even countries on how to balance energy needs with environmental awareness. With its headquarters in the rural west of England, ESD has expanded to set up offices in Edinburgh, Scotland; London, England; Sofia, Bulgaria; and Nairobi, Kenya.

ESD has built a reputation for helping newly independent and developing countries find ways to balance growth with sustainability. It has developed projects to capture solar and wind power and has helped London create plans for using renewable energy sources in new building projects. An ESD-developed fuel cell should help electric vehicles stay powered much longer than they could with traditional batteries, leading to less carbon waste being spewed into the atmosphere from the use of petrol.

All of this might sound like non-profit charity work, but ESD has proved to be a growing and prosperous company. In 1998, it received the Queen's Award for Export Excellence, an honour limited to companies that have played a vital part in attracting trade and funding to Great Britain. Its combination of environmental activism and business success shows that companies – and countries – can achieve one of these goals without sacrificing the other.

Energy for Sustainable Development designed and monitors the roof-mounted solar panels of the new sports centre at the University of Gloucester. Such 'low carbon' features reduce fuel usage and lower heating costs at the same time.

Glossary and Suggested Reading

Aboriginals   the original human inhabitants of Australia

atmosphere   the layer of gases surrounding Earth and other planets

biosphere   the part of Earth and its atmosphere that supports life

conservation   the control and protection of natural resources

crystalline   very clear, like crystal

deforestation   the process of destroying forests and woodlands

developing countries   countries that rely on basic farming rather than on developed industries for their income

ecology   the science of the relationship between living things and their environments

endangered   at risk of becoming extinct

environment   the natural world, including land, sea, air and all living organisms

evolve   to change or develop gradually

exploited   made use of (often in a way that is harmful or bad)

extinction   when a plant or animal is no longer living or surviving

federal   in the United States and other countries with regional powers, relating to the central government

First Peoples   a term used to describe the people whose ancestors were already living in a country when the first Europeans settled there

fossil fuels   energy-providing fuels such as oil and coal, made up of decayed plant matter

globalization   promoting similar types of behaviour and business practices around the world

greenhouse gases   gases such as carbon dioxide and methane, which cause Earth's atmosphere to trap heat from the sun and raise the air temperature (the 'greenhouse effect')

habitats   the areas in which a living thing normally lives

ice ages   cold periods in Earth's history when polar ice caps expanded

Industrial Revolution   a period in the late 18th and 19th centuries when there were rapid advances in manufacturing techniques

marine biologist   a scientist specializing in the living organisms of the oceans

multinational   extending across many different countries

naturalists   people who study living things and their natural surroundings

nutrient   source of nourishment

ozone layer   a layer of Earth's atmosphere containing large amounts of ozone gas and protecting Earth's surface from harmful radiation

petition   a document, often signed by many people, making an official request

pollute   to make harmful or unfit for living things

precedent   an act or result that can be used as an example in the future

pre-industrial   a society relying on farming or food-gathering, rather than on manufacturing

protocol   the first version of a treaty before it is signed and becomes official

protozoa   single-celled, usually tiny, organisms

radiation   light and other forms of energy, travelling from the sun or other sources

recycling   collecting and reusing materials rather than throwing them away

Romantic Movement   an artistic movement beginning in Europe in the late 18th century and celebrating emotions and nature

Satanic   having to do with the devil (or Satan)

silt   very fine soil that is often swept along by rivers and streams

spawning grounds   the lakes and rivers in which certain types of fish breed

summit   conference of leaders or representatives

sustainability   able to continue without causing damage to the environment

transcendentalist   someone who believes that there is an ultimate truth that can only be felt rather than understood through scientific means

transcontinental   linking both sides of a continent

tundra   a treeless area in the far northern part of the world where the lower soil remains frozen all year long and where there is only low-growing plant life

Suggested Reading

Barber, Nicola. *The Environment: The Essential Guide to Saving the Wild*. London: Hodder Children's Books, 1997.

Burnie, David. *Endangered Planet*. London: Kingfisher, 2004.

Featherstone, Jane. *Earth Alert! Energy*. London: Wayland, in association with WWF, 1998.

Graham, Ian. *Energy Forever: Solar Power*. London: Hodder Wayland, 2001.

Litvinoff, Miles. *Water and Wildlife*. Oxford: Heinemann, 1997.

Web Sites

Energy for Sustainable Development (ESD) www.esd.co.uk

Friends of the Earth www.foe.co.uk

Greenpeace www.greenpeace.org

Exploring the Environment www.cotf.edu/ete

Index